do not let writers
fall in love with you

Saima Tazreen

BookLeaf
Publishing

Presentation by *BookLeaf Publishing*

Web: www.bookleafpub.com

E-mail: info@bookleafpub.com

ISBN: 9789357610582

First edition 2022

DEDICATION

To the one who showed me
How deep I deserved to be loved
When pain was all I knew.
See, one Autumn wasn't enough.
But it was a pleasure
To have my heart broken by you.

The Glitch in My Matrix

Someday I will write letters to you in dazzling script, each dripping with immortal memories; till my fingers bleed from the weight of all the words we were too afraid to say. I'll burn them in flames of our favorite candles - reminiscing the warm, cozy blanket of your voice keeping my soul alive.

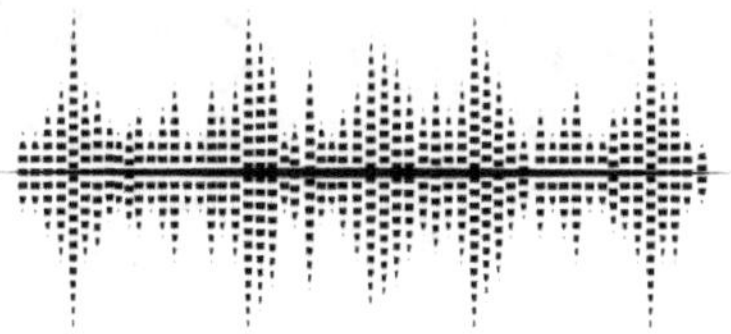

Regrets in the Horizon

We'll be watching the sun set deep into the farthest reach of
the horizon -
early wisps of cool twilight raising goosebumps on our bare
arms.
Wondering…
why our shattered hearts still long for each other's sleep
deprived voices.
Wondering…
where it all started to fall apart.
Wondering,...
if regret would have hurt less.

From a Distance

The days we spent hours talking; nights where your voice was the solace to my wounds; moments I watched your eyelids crinkle with barely hidden mirth - how can my soul ever forget what has been engraved within its walls? Someday we'll finally meet, and you will be watching me dancing in the drizzle, pearly white snowflakes clutching at my flowing locks. Your heart will be crashing through tidal waves of emotions you shouldn't express. Tears won't be enough. Screaming deep in the woods won't be enough. Maybe then we'll realize that loving from a distance was easier. Maybe finally meeting someone you have loved unconditionally will shatter the illusion you've been carrying around.

Soul of a Stranger

It's funny how the world is composed of exquisite poetry, but rarely are those written for the ones that belong to us. The crooked smile, the melancholic sparkle in their eyes, the lapse in their breathing when they feel an inexplicable rush of feelings for you - you'd think it would be easier to notice these things in the ones we chose to love. But is it? We notice every little bit of perfection in our star-crossed lovers, strangers on the streets, even people we have never met. We memorize them; we write pages full of poetry for them; we paint galleries of their beauty. Really, if our muses were the ones we actually ended up with, the world would be a very mundane place indeed.

Star-Crossed

5

Sometimes all love takes is a moment; an hour; a second. You can feel it. Calling you from the marrow of your bones, from the depths of your existence.

Haunting, screeching, yearning....

And then there's you. Even before we met, I felt you; like we have spent many lives together. As though, we have found each other over and over again, lifetime after lifetime. And maybe someday, in another reality, we will find each other, yet again.

Amber to Ashes

I never could point out the exact moment, but within the darkest hours of Fall, I was listening to you, and somehow I was in love. Basked in the madness of it all, I lost myself in the words we shouldn't have said. See that's what happens when two writers spend hours together, yet never meeting. Each word became a work of art, dripping with the emotions we couldn't avoid; a thunderous cyclone formed from two souls crashing flawlessly into each other. Blissful denial shredded through me - screaming and panicking with the excruciating inevitability of heartache. I wanted to believe that when you finally looked into my eyes, you would find me looking at you like nobody has ever looked at anyone before. And that moment led me to be in both: love and pain.

In the Future

I keep telling myself that we met at the wrong time. Maybe years later we will run into each other at a quaint little cafe somewhere, me sitting with my box of paint and you with a book I had recommended. Maybe then we could give us another chance.

Reminisce

I lean back, close my eyes and let the memories flow; the warmth of your embrace, whispers brushing against my earlobes, the throaty laugh that kindles goosebumps within my heart. The taste of your skin burns deeper within my lips as I marvel at the rhythm in your poetry practiced voice. And each time, the sensation of puzzle pieces falling into place with perfect harmony enlightens the unexpected comfort of your presence. The clock takes a pause as I reminisce the unceasing softness of your lips against mine. But, the juxtaposition of sadness and euphoria doesn't escape my ever ironic mind as I make the choice to walk away.

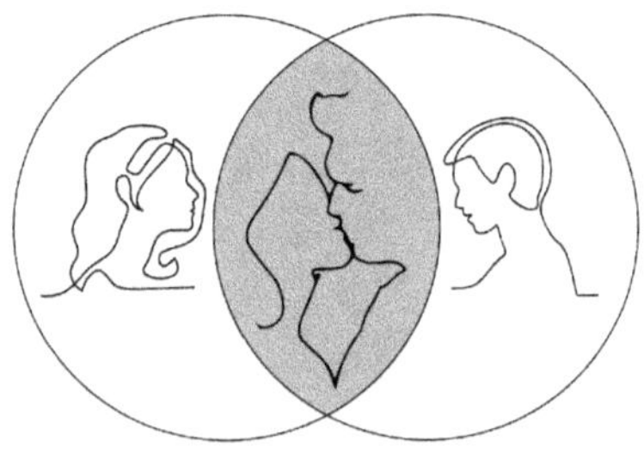

Do Not Let Writers Fall in Love With You

Do not let writers fall in love with you; because once they start writing, they will bathe pages in intricate letters, simply to depict your laughter. They will observe details you never knew existed within yourself, find words to make falling feel like flying, trace chaos within the depths of your inner peace. Their words will haunt you years later, materializing into your dreams.

Do not let writers fall in love with you; because you will live forever within their script.

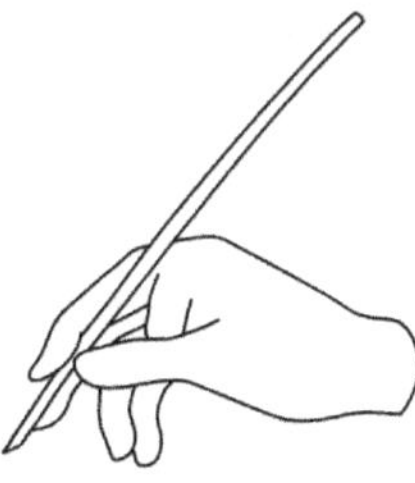

Healing from You

You were a lesson I should have learned
Even before I was taught
Since I had been here before, years ago.
I'd forgotten the pain that comes after
For I had loved when I ought not.
My heart had just learned to mend
From the scars it had long borne.
How would I have known
That it would be broken yet again?
Back then, I wish I knew,
That I would soon be healing from you.

Soft Place to Fall

The clash of our souls had long been written in the stars. You have stolen months, but there is so much more left to say. As the memories kept flowing, I kept searching for a soft place to fall - among the feuilles morte of past Autumn.

Long Enough

One day, it hits you. It's been long enough.
Locked in your permanent dance with temptation,
you let the puppet master pull at your strings.

It's been long enough.

Long enough that you've kept signing up to get your heart broken.
Long enough, that you have become tired of the irrevocable bruises in your soul. Long enough to realize that you are the very chain from which you cannot escape.

It's been long enough.

Burning Love

There will be days when your heart will feel like it's being ripped to shreds, as though a raging, hungry beast is pulling you apart by its teeth. Your breath comes in rasps, and you remember. You remember the day your soul had been at peace for the last time. And for some of us, the best way to manage the pain is to push through it. We lose ourselves in the hopeless attempt to write things that burn.

Winter

14

Today, I finally let it consume me
the pain of losing what never was.
I let the tears burn
through months of frosted memories.
And now,
you will only see Winter in my eyes.

Palette of Letters

That's the thing about art - the best ones demand to be seen during our worst moments. The empty echoes of a letter to unrequited love, teardrops falling on a palette of chaotic colors, a perfumed candle concocted with the redolence of heartache are simply pleading to be felt. As the memories turn from sweet to bitter, you ask yourself if the midnight madness was really worth the crushing weight on your chest. It becomes more and more difficult to breathe. And through the pain, you continue to create pages of soul-crushing poetry.

A Year Has Rolled By

As the world caramelizes into pumpkin spice yet again, memories of your words laced in blood and honey etch deeper within my heart. Wrapped in the melody of your voice, I became music; and with every burn, you became my lyrics.

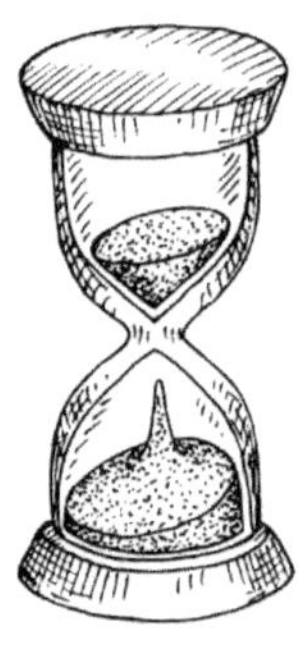

Grateful

I am grateful to have a heart that loved you in more ways than you ever loved yourself. If you only knew, it took every ounce of me to let you go.

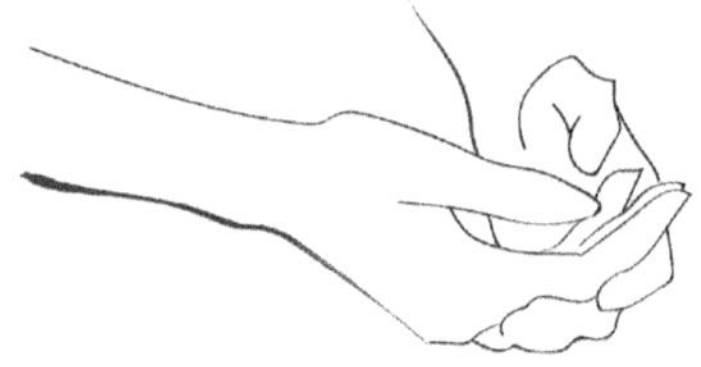

Words are All I Have

Every fiber of my being wants to be loved. Pieces you ripped apart want to be stitched back into a whole. But I've healed enough to know when my heart's on the brink of shattering, broken enough to never let myself fall back into you. Infatuation is too shallow a word, and I love words.

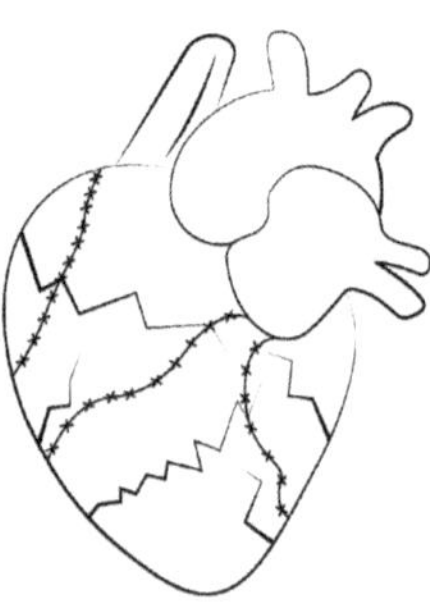

Bleeding Heart

And each time I remember, droplets of ink bleed through my pages as I attempt to love myself out of the darkness of your existence.

Ottawa

I am slowly rising in love with the crimson sunsets in your city. I no longer taste the ocean on my lips when you appear within my literature; I don't see your face among strangers in the streets anymore. The ghost of your voice fails to warm the ice within my soul as I learn to shoo the madness away.

Your Utter Ordinariness

As I put down this pen,
I am drowning in the flood of our memories.
And yet,
I struggle to remember them.
For now,
You have become a caricature of utter ordinariness.

www.ingramcontent.com/pod-product-compliance
Lightning Source LLC
LaVergne TN
LVHW020744160726
843364LV00075B/1492